MW00629150

The Lives of a Spirit

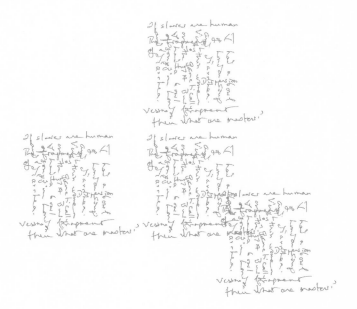

Glasstown

NIGHTBOAT BOOKS   BEACON, NEW YORK   2005

The Lives of a Spirit

Fanny Howe

Glasstown: Where Something Got Broken

© 2005 by Fanny Howe.

The Lives of a Spirit was originally published by
Sun & Moon Press in 1987.

Library of Congress Cataloging in Publication Data

Howe, Fanny.
   The lives of a spirit ; Glasstown : where something
got broken / Fanny Howe.
      p.   cm.
   ISBN 0-9767185-1-0
   I. Howe, Fanny. Glasstown. II. Title: Glasstown.
III. Title.
PS3558.O89L53 2005
811´.54—DC22

                              2005011406

Printed by Thompson Shore, Inc.

Handwritten pages by the author.

Text and cover design by Tim Roberts.

Contents

The Lives of a Spirit

White Plate Painted with More White

There was no mist on such an icy shore. The coast was a crust you could see at one glance, and a hard wind barreled over the sandy soil. Rusty war crosses tipped northeast. She was racing aimlessly now, purposefully then, away from the path she had tracked to the rocks.

A forgotten name moves in such fitful waves, engineered like tumbleweed across the mental floor.

Fringed and furred with frost, the white waves rushed in and out of each other, and violent crests shot brine into the air, as if shucking off excess emotion. At night the funeral wreath blew down to the sea—long yellows and pinks, birthday colors—lashed to the slimy black rocks. A dream smell of salt and acid, like the inside of a mouth, and I was down in it. Beach houses were battened shut, short pastels with torn screens, and always on my left, the heave of the night sea.

Barnacles bit my bare feet and knees, and greasy seaweed made me drop into tiny pools of kelp. Soft sand in those wet shapes there. This was the other side of the cemetery that domiciled on the top of a gnawed cliff.

The baby might have been the least worthy of earth's materials, lacking hardiness as she did. It lay with its ankles crossed and its arms spread wide, like one who lives by her feelings. Nostrils are always placed in front of the mouth, but this baby's lips, at the service of gum, tooth, and voice, protruded pink and soft. The application of her small fist to her lips made her, in all cases, the object of maternal desire.

No one could doubt that this was a model something. Every part of her seemed extra, more than intention could handle, and raised the question: Is the body made to fit the needs of the soul, or vice versa? Since her heart was a seething fountain of blood, people longed to lean their ears to her chest to hear those sinews at work. Her damp skin, soft as a rose petal, was sweet to the cheek. And when she smiled, the world was all confection and air.

They surmised that she had floated from the stars in the navy blue sky. Like rain at sea and no one to see, the coherence of these events and conjectures was never going to be accounted for. Now nested in sea heather, the baby will, later, learn her tens and alphabets on a pillow in bed. And will sometimes wonder: Little word, who said me? Am I owned or free?

The Portions of the Poor

She chewed her braid and waited for her mother. Snow bulged over the feet of the bench and patches of blond and blue-eyed fluff were flung like glamorous furs across the walls. Work-bound women walked awkwardly toward the trolley tracks. Skimpy boots, bright-colored coats, and in their round faces, a look to say: It's more than worse; it's better!

With a rush of rubber on asphalt, accidents erupted on streets nearby. And near where she sat, a sidewalk tool turned up a smell of porridge. From that vat of boiling tar the smell ran and entered those two small nostrils, filling her entire sensory body with longing. The years, whatever they are, had worked this transformation.

She had eaten as much bread at as many tables as the story of her luck would tell, but she was still feeling empty. She opened her lunchbox and looked in: a hard lump of bread and jam smeared out of a sticky pot, where the red seeds were burned from the sun. Cheap jam. This amounted, nonetheless, to "bread from Heaven" as long as she had a body to feed, or a dog.

She munched the bread and envisioned a plate from her mother's house: Imperial Ming, this white plate was painted with more white, snow, and cherry-red, hairlike branches. There was a bridge from blank to blank, floating.

And she remembered her mother. Once, close on the earth, she lay down, making wings with her arms moving up and down. She scattered her books, bag, and strap on the pavement, while I wondered: Why does she love where she was, but didn't?

And why am I where I am today? On my stroll around the park's pond, I asked questions like that. Confusing it was—the way the world ran back from every step I took. Even the stones leaped back, and the wiry trees, not toward a nature I shared, but from fear of my desire for that nature.

The dog barked ahead of her. There were sled tracks, next to the orderly print of bird claws, dog paws and garbage lids. And the light rarely changed, this part of the globe, from its transitory morning tones to one more blasting or benign. It might have to do with the city, its industry, air-waves, exhaust, and the fatigue all this brings to the ozone.

She looked to be waiting, lots of the time, to be consumed from the out-side. Since you can't, in fact, gain access to the surrounding phenome-na, you wait till they gain access to you. You move around, waiting for them to take over—bad idea—and to induce such complete control of your senses, you will at last be owned.

Her children have all grown up, like benchmarks by whose elevated states she can judge her own diminishment.

But she still can see her mother, as if it were happening right now, paused at a window, waiting for the tangerine sun to drop off the tree of Heaven into the night. The starlings have gathered in the bare oak and elms, and the sparrows hang in the tangled branches, the palmsbreadth of a baby, each black. They chatter like tambourines. Since birds have stayed on in the city, we must, of course, feed them. But of food she might say, "You are adding matter to nothingness.

"Faith keeps me young, and my attention, which is really hope, is prepar-ing my soul for the feast of eternity. This I do by looking at everything and trying, in a sense, to eat it all up. The mind has a mouth, too, which is insatiable in its hungers. While it is out hunting the visible, you are waiting, quietly, to be consumed by the opposite."

"Your father's gone down from the park and into the forest. No smoking, now, where he's at, and no dogs too. Papa wanted you always to be in training for that longest of sleeps. For him that training was the purpose of this life."

The grave markers of other fathers, by the way, tipped and grayed like a mouthful of rotten teeth. If the snow was trying to clean them, it couldn't. But gale winds, blown down from the Artic Circle, moved the stuff around, so it shifted its skirts like that many loaves of flour, to show, still, you can be moved by the unseen, if you see what is moving.

Mothers, fathers, motivator! The architecture of American socialism was an emblem of the gates of Heaven painted on the plate of Earth. How come it's so empty now?

As I crossed a small bridge, by the way, I noted that even this confined landscape changed dramatically from curve to curve. The snow looked like a finished job, undone. What a picture. The sight of the pond only brought salt to my eyes. Leaping, pleated. It had been there all along, so, at the edges of things, moving, waiting for a witness perhaps. The sapphire water is the mirror image of matter longing to fly. Cold water tries so hard!

It's like these women out there, here and her. The female body, which is a carrier of past and future, proves that a growth measured by roots is equal to roots measured by growth. Talk about trees! That's why the vague look, the drift of the lids off to the side, the slight pucker of lips and sporting handgrip on a child's wrist. They are half here, and half gone. They are the product and the consumer, owned and owning. They look hungry, which makes men ask, What more can they ask for?

Such enormous desires and such limited returns! Only repetition breaks the edges, saying, A soul can't split into parts, but is a part.

Once I looked at my mother look at her children eat. They all do that. It's often here that the path of justice begins, leading the women on, her first tasks done. Stinking of art and infancy, she weaves through random offerings, honestly trying to protect what runs away from her. If the child slams his sled into a wall, she will still leap forward, howling down at the unfairness of chance. She wasn't there in time. And this is the importance of her bad posture. Labor, fatigue—all for justice.

See how good the people are, doing all the little things we are famous for; This must be G–d's home away from home. Yes; no; yes?

Even This Confined Landscape

One morning around four she peeled the skin off an apple beside the warm radiator. On the windowpane, etched in frost, were leaves and thorns, silver flowers and daisy banks. She blew them apart and peeped out at the day. The sky was clear since all the clouds had fallen to earth in cold clumps, which scraping shovels now lifted up. She in her Levis and sneakers murmured, Is all this for children? Can I?

Mother, if I promise to return home without being forced, can I please take a quick trip? Please! My work place lies outside these gates. I must build a perfect park. Can I?

The human being is to her parents what an Eden is to a dual nature. "You can, but you won't," said my mother for her own reasons. "As soon as your wish can come true, you have already fulfilled it. I personally think the world is six hours short of paradise."

I ran with a closed Asiatic face. Useless fragments fell off like scales. A cold wave ran under my feet like a bamboo surface, as I pedaled across frost maps, round globes of ice, seeking the five spiral wheels that enter the gate to G–d.

Structures do variations on the same law, then comes the alchemist's mind and all is changed. My shadow seems to be the same shadow, wherever I go, and no matter how fast I move.

So what's the excitement? Surprised that the two you's are always together? In some unknown month your skeleton will weigh the same as everyone's. Thick-ribbed ice and chilblain hot as pepper will shudder you right down the air to Nova Zembla.

During her travels, she carried her bicycle through each park skillfully, hopping on and off when she turned sharp corners. She could often be found leaning the bike on her inner thigh, surveying, with her helmet unstrapped though still covering her bobbed hair.

When snow was imminent, meridian light whitened the pavement. Crosses and branches caught the attention of her quick bleak eye. Every thing was in the way.

When she wasn't tossing on her pillow or sitting on the foot of a couch in darkness, she was moving like this around the city parks. Blueprints besieged her as the morning star rose over the crests of the buildings with slow-moving satellites and airplanes. Irregular architecture, mossy in color, was the make of the neighborhood. Some latticed windows and stone porches, slate roofs and chimney stacks. When she rode to each park, followed by the question, Can you really build a peaceful place? Her will bent itself double and zoomed. She was fueled by that small question and said, Yes.

From any place she imagined landscaped courtyards, galleries where peo- ple could get together and joke, a square for parades, a winter garden, a theater, a church, and a resting place for military and solitary. There would be refreshment pavilions, including public toilets, for working peo- ple and children in an area studded with bowers and awnings. Was it Eden or Jerusalem, a socialist city? Even a communal cemetery was made of plain unmarked stones under a shade-tree.

And listening in the dawn hours to the radio, it's exactly that dazzling jazz she'd climb up on, the inverse order of tunnels in air. These were the verities of daybreak: a lake of gold with blue clouds building varieties of mountains—the idea of Heaven.

Like that the solid black trees seemed to beg and twist to get off this thing. Because of the weather I could never move from home. This, too, is an erotic shaft. Is it a sin or a trigger? It does shoot me up the notes, rung by rung, and G–d burning before. The nursery crib, natural wood slats with colorful decals of bears and balloons, remains my favorite bed. In it I can lie and watch the theater of the weather parade as days.

Once I was sitting on a bench making phalanx out of the chaos of the city. A bench is a kind of crib, after all. And I thought I saw communard coming. My fingers twisted a bit of costume rosary, a chaplet made of garnet and rhinestone. I swept the masks for one of him. But he'll never find her. Not that one. It was wrong.

Exteriors become rutted and dimpled. Depressions finally shade what once was smooth as the plump white back of a duck. She eats fast, from the pan, with her fingers, but will never be filled. Disappointment becomes the one appointment you can count on, likewise.

One time the flush left her face; she saw the perfect park. Like a field of lighted jack o' lanterns under a dawn sky, the topes and hummocks in the cemetery seemed to release orange auras. Peace! Quickly she whispered her insight to Heaven and moved away from the place like an independent traveler who is forcing her reluctant body to move through foreign streets.

She felt like a face in an illuminated manuscript, who couldn't get off the beautiful page about G—d.

Rushing home she passed the office where the paper green Xmas tree was weighed down with gold bulbs and gold trim and the women over their machines, humming. It reminded her of a green bench with small half dewdrops littering the paint. That was luxury's thought. If she had paused long enough, she would have thought only of the women themselves, their tedious labor.

At home begonia spat waxen petals pink against the haze in the kitchen. The chimney smoked like a tea kettle. A smell of bacon and toast had burned away the morning, the noon. Let her, now, pour tea and pass the little almond cakes with pink icing. She missed the other two meals and menus and it has started to change again outside.

Clouds have congealed into one giant snowflake whose stellar parts are spread from pole to pole. There is a yellowing around the edges, as with burned or old paper. The air champs at cheek and eyelid and plumes of smoke pour from the chimney stacks.

She pours the tea, and yellow jonquils in a thick glass vase are splayed against a window where the snow is now shown to be speeding, white on gray. It forms, first, a thin pocked surface, the same it will return to.

The community is moving around, waiting to eat and wash up. From the yellow jonquils comes a jocund melody: clarion and strings! The house is warm and Sunday would suit its atmosphere of genteel atheism.

If I had climbed up among the chimney stacks and the sampler city was spread out before me, I would have looked again for a park where nothing retaliates. There the small birds huddle heads under wings; the ducks waddle and squat like creampuffs around the whitening pond. The water squeaks into knots at the surface and settles. And the trees, still as granite, live for the light.

I would have said, Mother, stay at the window, but don't call me in.

The Verities of Daybreak

I settled on a desolate estate, bounded by high iron fencing spiked like a crown of thorns. On the palm of a marble statue was a small crescent-shaped wound, newly healed, and on the back a square wound, as if punctured by a naval shipbuilder's nail. It bled there from midnight each Thursday till Friday at an hour after noon, while the smooth white figure stared at a building as big as Versailles, but brick. It was a facility of some correctional sort. And I faced it, too, waiting for me to escape from inside.

When it happened, and I did, so happy were we to discover our roots were in each other that we were only able to think of celebration. Promptly we foiled the guards and trailed the city looking for some food. I prayed that all missing persons would be returned to their homes. Nothing but a chaos of noise and beggars when we huddled in corners, wrapped in threadbare clothing against a wind that smelled of the sea. We were certainly free!

This was the one when I learned that love comes in multiple forms. I learned it out of the ability to be happy. That there is love for animals, love for the seasons, love for music and art, love for friends and family, and there is the famous kind of love which comes in stories like the following: I lay prostate with giggles in the green woods. My bridegroom lounged on a mossy pillow. The warm sun camped on a ledge beside us and small flowers in that unmolested meadow budded and bloomed like fresh faces in a sultan's harem. Gnarled roots, lily of the valley, and dark red berries chafed against my crinolines and a flush came to my face.

I had prepared for penetration with the aid of night-scented gardens and their earthly perfumes. My fancies I had written in the dirt around the facility, although my groom once gave me a lump of beeswax, a leaky pen and a marble-covered notebook to play with. It never entered my mind that things were valuable. A deer was crouched in nearby needles and reeds, like a smoky fire. I preferred to lay against his soft dun coat than to loll in the loins of my life's companion. What can you say, after all, about the silence of beasts?

Don't let them die! I suddenly cried as the night sent forth those shadows that announce erasure.

She could never seek—willfully—a place among the circumscribed, but only among the untamed. If she had superficially prepared for her nuptials like the daughter of Rockefeller and Cadillac, then the reality offered a monolith against which he could only raise a vain command.

Only in the forest's moonlit halls could he offer her sanctuary of a fireside sort. Drawing her, homeward, over the soft ground was difficult indeed. He curled his lip and tossed his laughs by turns, and only when he rubbed his temples did she feel he caressed her.

Still she begged him to return alone to his calm sheets and cultivate the germ of holiness in himself. Like chinks in old walls, his eyes in the gloom let some light through, but he began a discourse on the botany of American woods and fields, as if to seduce her home through his superior grasp of information.

It worked. My hand burns where you tucked it between your elbow and rib. I knew every level of being then—from bone to bare skin; and why love is so close to G–d and d––th. I've got to give it up or ask for the same again! Yet whenever I put out my hand for the heat, nothing but chill is returned like the cold pat of air off a wing. Or a cell key's ratchet.

She was far from a sensualist, I hope you understand, but she couldn't resist a bite in the spice of romantic love. Besides, she pitied him. The first time she did so, she was standing among pickle tubs and flour bins in a wine cellar holding Moselles and Clarets. She let him then and again pull her about himself like a martial cloak and sword, and all this, she sensed, was to console him!

Each time, like a crimson flower through whose petals the sun shone, she blushed and sickened. Pity longingly strained toward the empty heavens. The burden of emotion was temporarily cast off, only to be refilled again, soon, and then baby after baby came, and labor inside the facility, and she would have been a little child again but for the growing burden of her emotions.

Now no more the appendage of a family man, and all the children gone away; today I held a slip of paper into the gas flame just to see the blue flame sun under the steaming kettle. This was also a form of love. Toast and tea, also, make me terribly happy, just like the tortoiseshell kitten dashing by the blaze into the chill drawing room and back again.

When heaven is up and about, frost sequins the sheet of glass and spangles like so many rhinestone in the morning sun. Peacock blue and fanning. G—d's quills and brushes are simply the skyline of trees.

This is far from a sepulcher by frozen water, but I still can tell that certain love, like winter, can be a cruel and suffocating nurse. And I listen to a copper cowbell banging in the glassy arms of a tree, amidst snowdrifts and flying sparks, and even if I have put on time like a heavy coat, I know all of nature was made for children.

A Gap in the Crumbling Walls

It was a chill March dawn that opened and closed like folding doors, when I went to the lofty window framed by thick crimson curtains. Outside were ivy tendrils, clinging to black brick. Shoes, which had long been strangers to my feet, now pinched my toes. I wore a shabby camisole under my factory gray; once it featured violets in its frills. Now a sweat started on my brow as I looked across the bare graveled court at my path to work.

The verdure of the suburbs had sullied into a dreary scene, made up of soaking clouds. Wet road, wet fields, and sopping pebbles on the unrolled gravel. The brick building I occupied, just like my face, was invisible to me.

All I could see was the sullen and sooty sky and red branches poking out of the walls.

Rain had rusted the gate's hinges. I could hear it groan woefully as it revolved for passersby. I took one last sip of coffee from my black tin cup, put on my raincoat and soon entered the open air for my passage through the graveyard census. Name after name would accompany me through the gate and past a brilliant thicket of holly, more vicious for the rain that silvered its prickles. I followed, now, smooth-rolled paths and nodded and bowed to only two souls out for a stroll, talking. Like this:

"The soul exceeds the body, I tell you, and will—must!—continue after, perhaps to be born many times. The body decays and wastes, see, while the soul hurriedly approaches another form. Genetics has to be a stupid field. We only grasp imperfect conceptions. Face it. This imperfection causes us to sin."

A nervous joy animated her limbs. She wore a pupil's eager face. Though poverty was assigned to her by fate, she seemed to have volunteered for it. If her snail-like progress made her appear destined for the cloister, she had been, on several occasions, a ready target for the shafts of Eros and had had enough of rules to sense the relief they gave.

Are eyes made to see the world, or is the world created for the eyes to see? She pondered this daily as she crossed the same path on her way to work, or cycled up the broad avenue of shops. Someone wanted to know what the soul weighs; to prove the existence of G–d through measurements. It's an old story. Like all jobs, nothing was ever added or taken away from what was already there. Things were recycled, rearranged; but you kept returning to the job anyway, just in case sufficiency failed while you weren't looking. Sufficiency is the law that causes exhaustion.

Finding a nook screened by trees, she sat on an iron bench beside a new-carved grave. The black turf was turned over in even folds: preparation for the least domestic bed on earth! She kicked off her shoes and her tears, like moonstones, dropped from her eyes. It wasn't pity. You don't hide a jewel in a pile of diamonds, but in lesser materials.

The fact is, she was ashamed of her own imperfections and purified her stains through bitterness and contrition of heart on these solitary walks to work. Knowledge of self and hatred of her thoughts and passions produced dread both of G–d and of man, when she was in this mood. Now she spotted a gate into the moldy wall and walked about twenty rods, her sorrow aggressive. A blank-browed statue seemed to suffer when she passed. Like eyeglasses lying on a table, she was all prose and lesser for it.

A mild dusky wind in the treetops lifted her gloom from herself. Ahead she saw threadlike paths through the forest and hedgerows black as sea-nettles. Her shadow trembled, as did her soul, twin children who lived, enjoyed, and suffered in unison. She was tempted to leave her accustomed path.

Certainly it is better to take a chance than to sink in a tempest of moods. Jail can be made with the fingers over the face, if the poetry is elsewhere and poverty here. Likewise, a glittering but vacant boulevard can appear to be filled with alien faces from little lights snapping and shining alone.

The crows sat in Sabbath stillness along the telephone wires. In the gray and russet tones of winter, it was hard to spot ducks on the water. But she saw a hatch of them out there on an oval slice of ice, eggshell blue. There the stone walls were stuffed with snow. Vegetation had ceased and the shroud upon the sleeping earth made her shudder. A strange dog barked at the paws of the beech trees.

Success is as "fixed" as any work of architecture. Throw down the dice of society and you won't be surprised at who does what. Those who can, do; those who can't, don't. All attempts at palliation will end in a frenzied shout. No. You can't change the effects of the economy, which sits with the composure of a justified veteran. Some people live on composure of a justified veteran. Some people live on macaroni and coffee while others eat steak from the grill with a bottle of Beaujolais. It doesn't mean taste is at work.

Just as perfection consists, rather prudishly, in the number three (measure, number and weight), injustice has the strength of disorder.

She whispered these lessons, by the way, aloud and moved back toward the enclosures. Take my remains to work and animate them, she said to herself.

In the waferless state, our failures stalk us like crazed spouses. When we gaze into that which stares back and sees, we are what we behold. You taste and are swallowed, too. And when you're in despair, worms, snails, and slugs seem to be your most intimate companions.

When the sky began to streak in lemon lines, she picked up a cold clod of earth and hurled it into a dirty pool of water. There, before her eyes, she saw the shapes of the nearby industrial section of the city: Titanic shadows of factories, chimneys belching false smoke, closed courts and streets, sulphurous skies and oil refineries lighted in dots as on a graph. Railroad bridges were slung low to the water, their lines brightened by graffiti. Mud slid to the water in stunted, crooked skids. A red umbrella was embedded there, along with assorted cans and runny metals.

Yet for the worker, even such a Gehenna, if income is there, is an acceptable system. Though no love and no individuation can be found, and a chill vacancy hangs about, at least she knows where she is hidden. In such grime they say the most precious stone is found: A gem that colors the dark and in light is possessed by light. If—during breaks—she has no teaspoon and tongs, no silver cream ewer or muffin under a plated dome, she has a community in anonymity, stones among stones and sparkling.

Back inside the large brick building she saw a shimmer of rubies shower the lattice from sun piercing the thunder-clouds. She heard a jet roar over-head, aiming west. While her boss paced, she chipped at her pencil with her teeth and fidgeted.

"Light my cigarette," he commanded. I stood on the tiles then, trembling and flicking the lighter, and I saw a whole ocean of flame rise gold and red before me, covering a good portion of my vista. Between heaven and earth, nothing but this wave of heat. It was no dream.

This man instilled his principles in me with a flash in his black eyes and a cloud on his bony brow. He was like a compound that cannot rise to the top of the retort without help. Yet someone else has to know the secret of powdering this compound in order to raise it, and that secret he keeps to himself like a perverse alchemist. Blessed is the person who shall find her own special function flowing from one remarkable notion, and who shares it. But even in this fortunate case the ego behind the ego is unable to identify the consciousness that had the sense to follow that notion through! Only the sharing is a comprehensible form of seeking the answer to this remarkable event.

My first husband rarely gave me blows, but always reasons; like the boss, no kisses but counseling. He was not one to eat with his drinks. No gluttony, but like the tapping of branches against glass panes, the ice always rattled in a glass when he held it. I wore dark nunlike clothing but my hair was ripped at the tips where old elastic bands had been cruelly pulled away. Few saw a girl so frightened giggle so much!

He had his suggestions, but the idea of making love to a doll or dummy was abhorrent to me; of clasping a creature made of wax, plastic, or wood in my arms—horrible. I dreamed instead of one in whose palm I could place my bare foot and be raised over the stone walls.

My infantilism led me to believe that institutions were protective! Meantime he wanted to watch me shop for silks and lace; he plied me with alcohol and terrible stories whose subject was Fear. "All true," he insisted. "If it could happen to me, why—"

I could taste the salt of Our Lord's sweat on my tongue at dawn, when there was an orange stripe across the back of the sky. I heard each passing car like a portion of wind, not strong enough to lift my invisible wings. I yearned for the eucharist, and this way to feel my spirit connect with a physical nature. This made his relentless theories puff and scatter.

When I told him of my appetite to taste and swallow The Word, he laughed like a failed tutor and a few stray ashes blew about my feet. Boys don't cry, but my innards sank in disgrace. He was amused by my ideals and said there can't be a shadow without a substance. It was then that he produced the substance: It was a portrait of himself!

I leaned against the glass window, with a dog's nose cupped warm in the palm of my hand. He began to attempt a general theory of mathematics and to relate it to patricide. I didn't listen but counted the rods from that window to the cemetery, wondering if there was a ladder lying in the short distance between.

Seeking Out His Face in a Cup

Her future, all in her, presented an avenue of gloom, as if to say, Go on, do what you can! All the lights in the crematorium were for her too bright, too hot. It was the usual pale light of autumn that improved her hours on earth. I moved the shadows when I lifted the latch, dragged the gate into the sun, and locked it with a gold key.

The length of the shadow was about six inches, which made the time close after noon. The shade lines lay like pipes, facing the water. I sat down and opened my brown bag. First I spread the paper napkin on my knees but it started to fly away. The top of the water rippled simultaneously.

It's crucial, I realized, in designing cemeteries, to keep the mathematics of shadows in mind. No one's going to fork out thousands of dollars for a vault that is shady all day. I pinned down the four corners of my napkin with each part of my sandwich so I couldn't eat.

She could tell her hands apart, with her eyes shut, even if they were rearranged. The position, though, of people she knew was random, if not the statues they had built around her. She was both adoring and indifferent. She had, then, everything to lose, being rich in the ability to be happy.

He had brutally judged her, but she absolved him again and again since the passion he had aroused in her was what provided her with steam for her flight. She could have consulted old texts in the library and found out the identity of the sin from which she sped, except there would be no mention of her, or him.

Papa's illness was a kind of contemporary furniture, a complete immersion in presence. He only knew that a female fiction moved about the ward; the links were missing. He saw shadows—he who worried about his work as if he had to save mankind!

At Cottage House, by the Charlie River, he dashed off a batch of letters daily. Out of the unwritten book of his imagination, and ink, a correspondence was created that many compared to perfume on the wing of an Olympian breeze. No vice was liked by him, but grace, youth, symmetry, and honesty. His favorite smile he dubbed "cynical."

I watched a sable stroke wobble on the pavement, a shadow of smoke really, from the dreariest chimneystack on earth. A marble angel had a smutty face due to the outpouring from that same vent. The predominant emotion of my heart was the dread associated with burning. I might have stood on a chessboard waiting for some hand to raise me.

My petitions were swallowed with each gulp of air.

It was a nosegay in a little straw basket—oil-stained pansies among fresh jonquils—which I once stood holding; and, later, a vignette of fresh wild blackberries shaking inside green leaves. But what am I to do with the citadel of time which stands between that she and the cemetery? I will, I know, rebuke the virgin who rejects the seeds as they are shaken from the ripe stem. My childish game of shake-the-pod-and-free-the-seed will, instead, occupy my hours. The world rolls around and around, and each day I take a walk with the weight of a man's spirit which pines for world-ly success, but crying out, I must help others!

That day I wore a white dress trimmed with black dogs. Long sprays of hawthorne ushered me into the shade, and in the back garden, bleeding-heart was enameled against the wall. A clash of bells summoned others to church, but I paced the edge of the carport with my basket. Papa looked up like Ezekiel staring into the oven of the sun. The muslin curtains were webbed in flames. The first to love is the first to lose it. With a slight bend of the head and a serious smile, he pocketed his property and returned me to the punishment of a false forgiveness.

At every next morning, I heard birds respond to the singing trolley and my illness made me sick; it made me.

One night near the apartment a shot split the air and signals boomed from north to south. The hunched figure of a shabby private stood by the table sipping a cordial. It was the purple zone, time for evening prayers where those who say them say them, the war was ended and the witty sally between the men quickly turned into whispers. I went to my room, a narrow chamber with pale blue walls, and pulled down my woolen stockings, which itched. I hated the shush of the sick room, so like sex and guilt.

I've never had luck in spooky houses. Under a slab in one of the passages a skeleton was half-modernized. In the primitive kitchen were a tureen of cold potatoes turning blue, a teapot, a dirty rag, a scrub brush, a tin of stale pecan sandies, and more. She was tempted to climb out the window, but there might be apparitions flourishing around the garden walls. Leaping dogs.

In her cotton nightie scattered with silk violets, she tilted into the hall instead, and, mute, listened. He was sitting on a stool near the passage and in that smoky room they hit out and didn't care whom they touched. Hilarity kept the truce of G–d away, and lovingkindness. He never flapped his wings, that one, but soared. She had told a horrid fib when she was just a daughter then. And her eyes of innocent light didn't account for any of it.

If she should grow up clever, he might like her better than her low-class mother; but she felt that cunning put bad blood in her veins, while she hid among dusty draperies and watched his progress. White fire sometimes blazed on the tips of her fingers—rhinestone stars sewed into her little costume gloves—and she sucked a finger until the cloth was drenched. She walked around in somebody d––d's old shoes. The white vote of uniformed salutes was raised above her head; she cowered, deliberately stupidly.

When she faked being a dog, it was always with her head down, her tongue hanging out, bruised and beaten from floggings. She climbed the padded stairs on all fours, panting. Explain why he distressed me so. Can anything cauterize these fears till they grow numb as air?

Her winter was like a scarlet box; the crimson curtains flushed and flickered and outside twilight was striped with the roots of bare trees; they were up drinking the sky. Don't worry about me, she would say without sincerity, I love a red window. There was suspicion in his face, but I had to ponder over its meaning. Why did I lie that day? An embarrassment so profound I pitied myself. But that's a sin. He *wanted* me to.

Always in cloister, park, or garden, the world seemed without photographs or newspapers, and the key put into her hand was the key to the canceled truth. Go. She should have been slapped or hanged for what she did; instead she was *sold*.

Now she heard a soft plash in the stillness and saw a monkish bird taking a bath in a puddle. In the pond the water was slow and tepid and some orange leaves were strewn across its surface. Nothing more could sink which hadn't already.

If she could scale Heaven to wear the consort-crown of a visionary, perhaps that would justify the droop of her head. She sat in a valley of rocks. When she stood up, as always she sought a gap in the crumbling walls. The yard gates were covered now with shade, and they creaked open, a heavy rusty iron. She would have preferred to exit through a tunnel of stones. But the grayest hours of autumn fail toward a kind of household light.

Escape from Inside

No context. But one gray day, and shadowless, I went off in search of a friend—another self, one who knew, as did I, that pain casts you down with your last belongings—necessity, body, and prayer. I wanted close association, and true trinity, the one who comes when you need it, and only when you've given up.

Despair-filled I looked beside a color mill. Ducks whirled around on a surface turnpool. The mill was distracting. It turned out all colors—red, orange, blue—which arced in air, over and over insisting on degrees of harmony. But at that moment beauty was of no interest to me. None.

Like waving a silver fork in a sunny room, the colored ducks began flying hither and thither as if to increase the distractions on purpose. I wanted in. The pink of a toilet from which a Venus might be born was not as alluring as the black of synoptic realism. To me.

I escaped their flutter by climbing to the dreariest place off the map. Down, through a manhole and ladder, to where the landscape is dark and watery, like a paddy here and a paddy there, but stonier than rice. My eyes were burning the last sparks of desire, when I found my friend, side-stepping an embankment. Two black mongrels followed her doggedly.

I touched her brow and asked what she was looking for. "A way out." She tossed her head to the left and I followed. The fact is, she always had a fever, and heart-poverty made her swift as a spider. It will do that. And if she ever wanted to see the fruits of her labor, she could only do so by not showing, but sharing them.

Even as a child, attic loopholes, seclusion, and oratory windows made up her interior. There, just inside the portal of a vault, flowers bloomed around a monkish girl whose bones were close to dust. Her few industrial dresses stayed folded there—a scarf, a sweater, black shoes—and when the basilica bells jangled like her chains, she lit candles in her refectory and suddenly worked on sums. That's when I looked in—not as a voyeur, but as a basic proletarian type, hard on labor and anxious for justice.

I couldn't help but notice that one of her interiors had a cheerful fire burning in a woodstove with an iron door and flying sparks. In this room she wore a pink dress, and silk stockings, expressing a modest lust for human love. That's hard. Lightbulbs flickered at her footfall here, as if the sky were raining bombs. So far from her was all flesh measured, no love would ever hover over her.

Beside us, the water was soundless and still, as if it were a river that you could step in twice. The dogs began to tussle, all in fun, and she, being the little daughter of the Torah that she was, met and parted them with an interpretation. It went like this: "The body is to its shadow what a war is to storms. All technology. That's the comfort of it."

I then trailed her up from under to where rows of poplars and limes unlined. Raindrops spattered sunken fencing, and she gazed upwards, like a child who is longing for a treat from her late parent. She said, "Peacemakers are the most valuable people on earth. Like pear-shaped pearls, their worth is beyond estimation. But the one who comes next will not be wearing a cassock or a scholar's robe, but a uniform!"

She was fixed on a far place, and I looked in to see her drift to her main room in a long bolster and stole, a head bandage and a veil, as if the thicker the swaddling, the wider the gate to grace.

Now, spitting a weed off her lip, she took her philosopher's stance, pensive against a tree. "I think, therefore I talk. And next I use a pen to prove the presence of our Father in language."

"Is this what you want?" She pointed to where some soldiers were stationed, worried about luggage and rattling pavements. Brown paper packages, steel lockers, umbrellas and all manner of weapons littered the stones.

Tall, but tender, one man's image I can see today. He worried, "Have you got any memory of me?" No ghost or angel stood before me, but something of each. Mutual scrutiny and each eye spoke. "Yes!" I lied, chaotic as a chicken. "Then why have you done nothing for others all these days?" he murmured and moved away into the flock of men. In a flash, the truth was on me; the soldier was being the Son of Man. And He was gone!

"But you have what you want," said my friend. "That is, the lie."

No contest. She was my superior. All my indulgences gathered and hung on my limbs, but she kept few relics in the path between herself and her beloved Father. The Light, the Life, the Word, made her flesh crawl. Obedience, like habit, makes time into a thing that you use. And the anonymous poor, whose labor is forbidden improvement, whose experience counts for nothing, gain an insight into time which has no haunt but chant.

She wouldn't follow me in to eat the Bread of Life, but chose to settle on the grass outside, while the westering sun blushed on her cheeks. She could tolerate no separation from those outside, and the vines that she leaned into received her slight weight. I watched her lift her slender arms as if to direct the sunrise.

The horizon lifted a skydrop: buildings out of dimension, cornered lights and the sound of bombs like "isms" and "ologies." I wanted to enter the embrasure of the institution, though she would stay outside.

Assuring me she would always wait, she placed, neatly a bunch of new-cut quills on a ridge in the side of a damp wall. Then she said our Father's image was a luminous print. And the problem of fitting her imprint to His was what the ink was about to attempt. She forgot me then, and wrote:

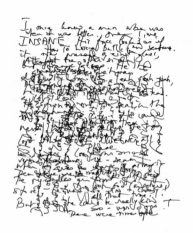

Crosses and Branches

I shall not be married, I suppose. Berry by berry and nut by nut, the tree will grow bare. Like a bird feeding its fledgling, the visionary clasp will first melt, then chill. And stately raindrops will fall on the long lawns, beyond the portions of the poor, myself hutted and hatted, face up.

The service is over. Will he look at me? No, and I grieve. Mute is my mouth, which can only speak the truth, or nothing. Probably I will be an old maid, asking, What was I created for? My children, after all, have grown and are gone. Still I long for something daily, to discover and to know like numbers. A man was never a thing to love, but an experience to have.

I visited its brink one twilight, it was like a certain old thorn, the kind that looks sharp but crumbles between your thumb and forefinger. My black apron was carrying roses toward a glass door. I was told he could never do with a talkative wife. In company he is quiet. It's a poor harbinger of luck who has no knowledge of happiness. I was not pricked.

I paused behind the monuments, and gazed toward the city lights beyond the rectory. If I seem hard toward you, while the stars gather and glitter in my eyes, it's because these indefinite abstractions put a shawl over my hopes. G–d of Heaven, be clement! Not often do people test the divine conflicts and come out prevailing in prayer.

See, I've had a suffering night! The whispering of zephyrs, the carol of crickets. I felt I was imprisoned in a drawer between shrouds and sheets, all folded and cold. If there was bread, butter, pastry, and salt on the shelves of my pantry, none of it could nourish the breath in me. A terrible dream seized me like a tiger trainer:

I was a little girl being shipped from America. We were seated at a table, the food like ashes on each plate, and he puckered his black eyebrows and smote his chest with the force of Demosthenes. The boat rocked to and fro. The elements were in a ferment: tempests and whirlwinds and mountains of waves on either side. The wind came almost wholly from NNE, and the sails were in rags. Oh Papa, save me and leave!

His smutted face engraved itself in my terror, as he thought I was happy! It was then that the water changed color, and apertures in the clouds gave glimpses of writings. My underminded structure sank into childhood. The boat grew wings and was flying like a twin-engine on a runway of sea.

This little girl sat in her chair, strapped, her face pale with suffering. She smoothed her hair under her beret, and gazed steadily through the port-hole into the stormy sea. A silk ribbon hung around her neck, and a gold chain—both in the repository of her jewel casket at home. She carried a little satin bag with a tassel of silver beads, and was the image of polar winter. He handed her a cookie, this man who was dangerous people.

Like the hollow tree or chill cavern, forsaken, lost, wavering, the little girl's expression. Then she bit, as if with the wild beast and bird, as if hunger and cold were her comrades, the green wilderness her mother, and as if she was chewing a juicy berry, or saccharin root and a nut. It was wonderful then to see the ocean turn into mossy banks, soft as pin-cushions and the pinions of the plane wobble and fly.

She was alone again, and free—all this expressing the force behind fragility. I woke and woke again, and went out to walk in the designated area. You can't make a diagonal path across any part of the grass here, but must follow the asphalt. Little wire fencing is looped along the bor-ders there, and so signs are unnecessary. When I look at a wire, or a knife, sunk into the earth, I know that one element accepting another is really saying NO.

Yet because I lived here, and had been instructed, I also sensed that this landscape wanted to represent the Messianic age. How? Each path was designed as if the next, at last, would represent progress; and each step was, paradoxically, drenched in the tangle and nostalgia of the old days. There were a good many rules driven toward field and furrow (don't walk on ice, don't stray and get lost) and none of them together has produced perfection of action in one soul. The pleasure of reliving old flaws may be irresistible.

Now when there's only a very small splash of disarray (a bent red tulip, a snap of thorns across the grass) and the rest around remains in order, you imagine that this disarray was meant to be! So, too, the human being is composed of intentional mess, of necessity, and the will. Misreading, buoys the spirit. I think every event is unpredictable.

Papa's rules are innate to his landscape; they force you to think twice. How can I scale that wall, never? If the watchtower man has his back turned, can I make a dive into the flume, and crumpled up, get shot? And it's only when you lie down defeated and dream that you experience a love that is frosted with hot lighting and colors, shapes and textures so trans-parent, they are apparitions of perfection.

In dreams you see through solids! It's Papa's way of showing you how to know G–d: with all your parts abandoned, cast down, while your spirit is free to move about.

The Mathematics of Shadows

Seven o'clock in the morning and it's impossible just now to understand the presence of the sky, of trees. It's like discovering that the void will not come in search of me one night; but more things.

Now I've already been told that I was a little distracted last night. It was, let's face it, difficult for me to be out among the raucous speakers and famous people, but if I don't occasionally step out like that, I won't remember why I chose to be anonymous.

I recall, at the end, one person saying, Don't be troubled; you will bear your suffering. I had a token, and so I left at once. But now I can see she meant to be kind, without offering consolation. The rest of the community moved back and forth, confused and bitter, as she went from one to the other with such lines.

Happy was I, then, to have a childish view of G–d. Like light on my hair, it was not an encumbrance. Many affections are, no matter how passionately held. Nonetheless, for one who accepts everything, I still have a lot of trouble swallowing it.

Sunday I took a little rest on a bench in the cemetery. You would not have seen such monuments in the Gospels, and my faith passed away once more in the shade there. No one heard my prayers, and I felt as if I were fishing with a line in that garden of stones.

After all, it's the same to the world whether I live or die, but not if you, whoever you are, do. Love your family, my friend; that's all I can say.

If one day I'm a cured girl, the beacon will announce my arrival to heaven's port and all the saints will be chasing me off the earth. You might say this life is my assignment, a great pain, especially if I compose pretty verses meaning nothing. I'd rather be St. Cecilia who got married without fear than to sit on top of a metaphorical column rhyming and tapping my toe in time to hidden bumps.

You don't often, by the way, come upon a perfect park. Mine is in November, late afternoon, and the elms are like stones. Only an accountable welter of yellow leaves slides through the air to the asphalt. The benches are brown, green, or cold. Along the rim of the horizon you see a glamorous tangerine dusk, and there is a wetness to the sky, both yielding and opaque.

There's another park I love and this one is a boneyard, for real, designed and settled in the 18th century. A very great effort has gone into making the area pacific. A mist like incense dreams the hillocks, hummocks, topes, and holes. Especially at daybreak, but also late at night, when you come to make out on the heaving grave beds.

We did. It was spring and the dose of lilac breath was the heavier for the late damp hour. We fit right into the place where they pour water into rusty tins and then stick the poor flowers in. Memory lasts a lifetime, tough as geraniums, wherever it begins. An angel played a stone trumpet on a tomb. It was a baby angel and it stood up against the black sky like a negative shadow. The moon looked disturbed as if something was in front of it. Light.

Rosebuds hit the metal, the way male and female try so hard to get back together. And when the G–d Hole spills substance from the sky or ceiling, it comes spermatozoic in size, speed, and absence of true color. Like sewing of the Milky Way, it goes XYZ. The funny thing is, it makes no noise and doesn't exist. The only thing you can learn from seeing it is that a piece of space makes contact with a piece of time, and because they are in constant motion, you can make two into one.

In that black graveyard, I became two hermits in one. While one got laid, the other prayed. My wildest testaments came under conflicting impressions, when I didn't refuse my mind anything. I wanted, always, to be other than myself, just the way it feels when you have lost an opportunity.

I also wanted to thread a machine, anonymous as one "who had no comeliness." But I couldn't contemplate the object, I was so taken by the meaning of the subject, and I became too casual with each task until it became like embroidering the silk in a casket. Who cares what it looks like in the dark?

If I weren't a slave walking in shackles, I'd kick like a baby in a bed, and simply delight in this place. After all, what's in that baby's head, rolling down the promenade? Iridescent as a marble, with an orange iris, any mind can roll around, illuminated.

I called my father once to ask: What is the meaning of life? Spare time, was his response. I feel, sometimes, that I am a little slice of time in conjunction with a lot of space, and not, indeed, the reverse. Those times I'm sure that's what he meant.

Other times I'm not so sure of that; not when I sweat with those suffering. My bedsheets grow salty as a sail tight full of wind and spray, while my mouth is parched and dry, when I imagine the torments of children and other innocents in pain. Then I think up some things to do before the world ends:

1. Get down on your knees and play.
2. Scrape the air till Heaven appears.
3. Go out and shoot all the violent people.
4. Get lost.
5. Kiss a lion on the lips.
6. Leave G–d with all your heart and all your mind.
7. Whenever you are moved by someone's suffering, take it into yourself, until you are miserable, and pray, simultaneously, that the other person will be relieved of his or her suffering. You'll feel a lot better, fast, and so will the other, as the suffering floats off on another course.

I walked close to the path's edge, where the shadows fell, testing my faith. The window of my cell was open. Everything looked like a disguise, and I cried, not wanting to be a floating mask. Were little angels playing tricks on me, I wondered, and I made an Act of Oblation to Merciful Love, promptly, my face turned up to the sun.

The fact is, I need artificial lights to see my little nothingness clearly and interiorly, because all the density of nature can be too harsh in an instant. Besides it is the thin glass on the bulb I am used to, and its fairy web inside.

Once, during Confession, I realized I was only wanting a full dinner of soup and bread, and not forgiveness, and all because I couldn't eat! That knowledge made me angry at physical nature.

I touched a periwinkle in my pocket and turned to the side to hear the priest more clearly. "Never turn your face directly to the enemy, and always be glad that He is no longer in pain." These instructions were beyond me, and I couldn't believe that any surface went all the way through. But then he said words of comfort: "Don't worry. Your price has not been raised."

All my windows seemed to fly open, and spring air swam in. Why do those flowers fail to open, I wondered, and this time my mother's voice replied:

"The poor child wants everything to happen at once. Seven, and her night-gown is cotton with a lace trim and pink silk flowers woven across her flat little chest. These are the flowers she wants to see bloom. Oh, oh. Her coughing, though, has stopped, and the spitting of blood."

A railroad carriage rattled by and a submarine foundered in a Pacific storm, slowing to three knots an hour. She blew out the light. It was not nearly dark enough to sleep, but there were luminaries in the box of Heaven, signs for time, and I knew I could sleep if unable to.

"She was afraid of the horns of a slug," my mother murmured, "but not of the glister they make. It can be a cure."

I'm afraid since then I've feared sleep like d- -th. But I'll push myself into it like a hand silverpointing in glass.

During naps, even as bombs are falling on the city limits, I often drop into G–d's arms, because I am fatigued. And then I have quite an appetite—for Heaven! It has to do with being a little piece of space coming in contact with big time. And at dawn, when the vines on our apartment wall begin to moisten and green for spring, I look at my reflection in the windowpane like a Sacristan seeking out His face in a cup. And then it's as if G–d calls me a doll! And suddenly my faith is only equal in depth to my doubt.

All the chestnut trees, with their white cream blossoms, curdle in the coming of the dark. Despair is like the hard glossy ball that comes in Fall on these branches and that loves the shadows.

I must be careful, therefore, not to cover myself with shadows or wings, but to remember an angel is primarily a messenger and must be very busy with the washings-up of whites and colors.

To be that little girl again, I am! And I can sit on G–d's knees, if I want to, and recount my loves and disappointments as they pass from my life. But naughtiness will enter my imagination, you can bet on it, and I'll be tempted to do something silly, and my guilt will last the length of a Credo.

Praise is not equal to a caress, ever, just as the silver spoon in a mouth is vulgar beside the silver thread of a spider's web. I have let things pass, too much, like a green grasshopper jerking over the blades of the grass.

If I could just get my little cell in order, they would let me out again. I'm ready to go out. Through my open window, I can see the stone bank along the pond, its serpentine curve beside the path, and beyond the path, the trees. My bench is there, where I sit with folded hands.

Dear A Brittle:

... were meant
... you from them.
... to liberate you
from them.

Glasstown: Where
Something   Got   Broken

The Sparkling Stone

When I was an infant I was dandled on the knee of a Nazi. Her dress was like white icing on a fake cake. I remember the feel of it. The smell of warm milk bubbled from the rubber she pressed into my lips. I was in my howling years and saw all ceilings as slanted. Her knees under my spine bounced until my cries were like a wedding between horror and error. No mother's milk but a series of rubber nipples.

Acoustics were my field of study. The path of sound was my liberation. By the time I had located it, I was part of it. If my screams came to nothing, then my silence did, for in it I learned to hear the music of others. I

remember there were two kinds of sounds in those days: metallic instru-
mental sounds and human ones; occasional booms. All these sounds
longed to overwhelm each other but remained separate and equal like
threads in a carpet. When I finally took note of another farther sound, it
actually freed me: birds, wind in leaves and rain on a tin roof.

I learned that everything develops in exact proportion to something else
that opposes it. I could measure my silence by the bumping noise around
it. It went this or that far. Whatever you strained for, you got. And then you
couldn't get it out of you again.

I couldn't be protected by people and expect to stay free of their influ-
ence. But when I first heard music (a whistle) it gave me a way to bridge
the gulf between instrument and world, and it was also the way to dodge
human influence. I let my mind run up and down the harmonies like a
sparrow on a wire. I don't know who the organ grinder was all that time
but he was there, out on a street.

In any case, music helped me control my terror while I was rolled
through the streets like a play slave in a wheelbarrow. I hummed. The
trouble is, a Dissembler's voice kept emerging out of radios and win-
dows like the noise of sipping straws in empty cups: *ku, klux, klan, styx,
stasi, swastika. . .*

Now legs were levers and hands incomplete wheels.

The white wooden house outside and the halfwhite twigs and beyond them a wall in line with things blue. The land could only be warmed by a west wind drift, it was so cold.

As a glass is always water in very slow motion, so an icicle was a reminder of how far we had come since the Garden.

Every first move was a hesitant move. Adam and Eve were poised at the gate from the Garden, their feet raised, the wrong feet first, in retrospect. Goosestep or misstep, the history that followed belonged in the category of permanent miscalculations. The original guess: wrong!

Is it the case that technology also took us far, far from warm bread while its nihilism showed that the past is all that is allowed to live? Face it. The minute the work is complete, it is obsolete.

While my aural attention was floating from room to room, my happiest nights were found in listening to human voices at a distance. (In the same way I continually pass others suffering, confusing their difficulty with a morbid dread of other humans like myself.) Time zones intersected on the slanting ceilings and dropped with the light. Under and outside, victims were dust under monkish stones. Some of them were still up and walking. Were people moving in order to shuck themselves? Shake off being?

I remember miles of bewildered children in knitted caps and mittens filtered towards some bricks. The snow was attaching itself to smoke stacks and branches, wires. Each one had a bone to pick with G–d. And meanwhile the cruelties made logs for cabins twelve to fifteen feet long and notched. These would store the children. Later the animals were given their roomy forest, those animals whose paws dapple the snow. They are always going or have departed. I was called Paul.

Rising by plane from the Netherlands, we children turned gray over Luxemburg. Snow in the spruce trees below flaked into handbills and pamphlets. Even the cinema system took part in the campaign to color the world gray. In that war each baby weighed a boot and bricked up, during those years, the good men's power dried up and their foreskin shriveled.

Trains were heading in all directions grinding over weeds on ice cold tracks. The wheels at 5 a.m. bore down with the force of seventy men on a muddy woman. Snow whirled airily against each brick entrance where humans tried to get warm from smoke and confetti. The litter in the trees was sometimes white and on the sides of streets it was thick and gray. The city was an oyster inside a pearl.

Can we avoid dying by making a plan for others to die ahead? Send them before us ruthlessly to scout out the territory? Or fill it? A hutch stuffed with woodcutters and chicken-killers was my birth place. I know it. I feel it. I remember it at the level of bone. Grass ate up through the foundations of barracks and community graves. In stone rectangular caves, potatoes were the food of starvation and baked in ovens with those who would eat them.

I did my research and found out that in May of that year there was rain in the ash trees. One interim peace agreement was complete while another country pulled its forces in and out of a hellish corridor. I felt like a toy doll while all this was going on. The radio warmed and cash registers rang in the season of The Dissembler. And images the size of my pink palms were lowered up and down before my eyes: St. Francis holding a lamp, a bleeding heart, and Joseph with the Child Jesus in the crook of his arm.

I had been switched from nurses to nuns. This signaled the beginning of my liberation.

Soon an armload of seaweed and pounds of fish gleamed around me in a country they called Homeland. Innocent Homeland.

Now I remember one woman knelt and the other stood in a square like an illustration in a children's book. Bright, shining colors on distant hills and the two of them cooking. Pumpkin soup, sole in dill, steamed greens, gingerbread, apple cider and chilled dry wine. Candles showed each face at the table filled with the expectation of a hearty laugh. By the time the coffee had come each had passed into a new position. I don't know why I was there, but the moment passed like happiness and then the sound of that happiness.

Strains of music. In the same way certain melodies bring my earliest childhood back to me, before I was taken to this continent. They are often followed by a surge of bile, palpable in the back of my mouth. At such times I am bowled over by the coexistence of beauty and injustice.

I know there must have been a day when a mother held me like the sun. Love is passive. It only hears and sees what it wants, and endures in a state of inaction, pondering whether to lift its will to go after the object of its want. In this way it can become confused with weakness.

Does a person or doesn't he direct his own life?

That's a tough question. Anxious to better our opportunities we sometimes lean too far and kill them. It is hard to be a man.

O Stands for Rebirth

But then I am not a man who is easily silenced. Instead I am easily erased or ignored. Shop clerks don't see me. Some citizens feel my benevolence but can't locate it. I am at a table either in a crowd of trees or a crowd of people, and they are interchangeable. None of them know I am there except from the sound of my laughter.

At the same time, life has been hard on me. I have felt its blows so acutely, there is not one area of my body that doesn't flinch at the approach of another person. I am all nerve and skin, my brain stem quivers. I am little for a man in the Western world. Colorless and wiry. My value is entirely in my aura, not in my muscles.

I spent most of my life as a celibate onlooker. Once I loved, and not so long ago, with a consuming passion that almost killed me. I loved so hard and so well, it made onlookers feel sorry for me. Humiliated, I nonetheless could not control my feelings for this person who was cold and white and whirling in a vortex of past history. The person could not flail back up to the surface, but submitted to a reiterative life passed in streets that were humming with memories.

It was my last love and ninety percent pity, a kind of divine and self-emptying pity; I would do anything to make this person happy for a few minutes. The contempt this kind of love engenders in others has many modern names. But the truth is, the person I loved was so degraded and so disgraced already, was referred to only in disparaging tones with laughter following, that it was all I could do not to turn into a nurse, to stroke, embrace and kiss that body long and nakedly. Pity is the form that late love often takes, as does the work of the aging artist.

The dust will blow over us all, but in the meantime all I ask for is a language that revives my beliefs.

I even enjoy the old revolutionary words like poverty, struggle, the people, the rich, down with and up with, and despise the new words of capitalism.

I am old-fashioned. Yet I trust the young—those between fifteen and thirty five who can still effect change; and children. What should I do while I am waiting around at the end of my story? I already passed the point when I was supposed to die and the doctors intervened with my permission.

The ideals of the twentieth century died (unlike me) exactly on schedule. God ate the people or the people ate God. That was the dual diagnosis given to us at the Millennium.

Many people tell me I look like the poet Rilke. Some even refuse to accept my denials when I tell them I am not he. The last time was outside a movie theater where his life was being played on screen. The departing viewers refused to believe I was not him, or the actor who played him. I am him and the actor who plays him.

What I wanted to say is that the word "two" is a joke.
That's why I am always laughing.

Cathedral Without Wheels

Sixties memories

bunch-punch

money-grub ~"

g 1, ~   groovy

gourmet garbage

chof f   *NA ST. VIINCE1"1' PIILLAY*

. , . a'~=; ~:3,',':-j:',•W•';' ..

;.

.   a;,c :cue. ~<=c .~,~•.

-       ~^.   .∴.? .   *E   s   ,~a_ed n*

slammer blow job

the pits'

flip   out,

bo   ob tube

john

sniff-test bummer

..~~groupie

zonk

ke   gu rls

Happy t e p ce aakers:'''-

t~1   rsl   d sonh y   all bbee ccal   sons ~ God.

My daughter's name was something she could never stand behind, and so it was also the first point of disintegrating identity. What she stood upon was image instead, not sound, and over the years she learned to die to the world by choice, in intervals (random and finite being) simply by watching everything that moved without will.

She could not be happy staring hard at a fixed object; indeed she could weep from it if she looked too long. But if she made the distance vague, it was okay. She lived then in the aura of impression.

As water seemed to be the origin for solids, so sound seemed to rush towards silence. Listening, she was an interior without walls, an insubstantial.

An experience that you dread having again, becomes the experience you dread all your life. Yourself.

Likewise, looking for a home near home was better than being at home. You might find yourself existing if someone recognized you in an actual setting.

To be alone is to prepare for your own erasure.

Travel was her promiscuity, she was very temperate otherwise. A splinter had found its way into her bloodstream when she was nine, and the pain radiated pleasure into her hand. Only by using her hand productively could she locate that pleasure and bring a numb world to life in her body.

Our forefathers were millers who sold off their daughters like reproductions at a poor man's auction. Protestants. The spirited girls were given away to men, and the churn of the mill went on cutting. Foam stuck to the falls, but leaves like fish bellied up on the surface of the water.

Pain makes girls useless. After she was sold, she stood behind windows.

The way a sealed maidenhead wears the face of its owner, she felt her eyes in every cell of her body. Why be anywhere at all, she asked herself.

Then she concluded, I might as well be here, since I have to be somewhere.

When people found her and invaded her secret world, she learned to become lighter and airier by giving away everything she had and everything she wanted; she had few desires in the end. She liked cheese, bread, water and wine. She liked one man at a time, usually in her mind alone.

I her father got lost in the woods when she was very young. I had gone to get some fuel and strayed into the dark part of the park. Usually it was children who did that, but as she sat waiting for me to return, it dawned on her that I had taken the spirit from her with me in order to be as intuitive as she was.

Until this hour the conditions of being in the world, no matter how strange or painful, were acceptable. But after I went off with part of her soul, she could not stop waiting for me to return. This waiting helped blind her to the oppression of institutions. She endured them patiently. Even buffalo brown buildings and human spaces that included selves. If tea-drops burned on her wrist during breaks, she didn't feel them or flinch.

She might have been composed of material as biodegradable as a paper bag. Once I pinched her, just to see, but she had no self-involvement like that. She was like Tinkerbell dying on a wall. Her spirit was losing and creating steam.

Like a sailboat floating on the horizon an inch above the sea, she now remembered the messages I sent her before leaving. That is, she put pieces of words together as if they were members of her fractured soul.

Keep at it.
You will achieve nothing.
Just keep at it.
Suffer.
Love on, even though the one you love (me) will disappear.
Give everything away.

Not one psychological term! As she reconfigured her interior like a spirit pasted to the inside of her skin the world became all matter, matter, matter and science was the last source of wonder. The gay dance of planets and comets, fireworks and splashes of color—the universe in an orgy of delight—these pleasures, she came to believe, were supposed to be magnified by the human soul. Why was a human being so unyielding to happiness? Eros lost. Was it her father's fault?

The Dark Part of the Park

It's just an idea but it looks as if I have disappeared and survived. I now stand pondside. The steam is never whiter than at night. Every puff tamed. Ducks make a splash at 4 a.m., then punch their quacks back into their bills. Fleet lightning off the screen. There is a gardener in the grave-yard dignifying paperish flowers with clippers; he is my forefather.

White boys careen and brutalize the atmosphere; it was an error. I hear them and know who they are even when I can't see them. Their quality, their violence is a form of nationalism and optimism. Everything they do is bursting with confidence. They don't sense my presence. I am a

Nowhere Man.

Fringe-fires in the electric lines. So as to be homeless and invaded by outer space, I went into a forest, leaving my daughter behind. It's normal to want to be free, but that wasn't why. Passed away, more, from that particular territory of authority. We were squeezed between two wars but I don't remember what they meant.

I like to tell men who beat up women and who shout at their children that even so, their victims are free. I know this is so because the line between genitals and rage is always open and free. I saw some Muslim men rolled up in paper once and their mothers cried, Such beautiful children!

Here is a notice: Mr. Thigpen will serve you lunch today.
Humans take pictures of animals in order to remember how to be moral. Some are sitting in a hotel called Cathedral Without Wheels, or is it a place of worship? Is hell? Is television? Clip away at the telephone bill, don't pay it all at once, make sure the plutonium is safely packed under the sink. Don't talk fat in front of slobs, but diet in secret.

There's something as dull as concrete and building sounds out there. I hear the thud for hours and can't manage a shout. I imagine a tangerine, veins, juice, compartments inside dimpled skin. Fruit is free on the tree. If I think this, it will soothe me.

Who not to kill? Is this the world I made or all the men before me? Mortar concocted out of babies and crushed slaves? Did money win the war between numbers and words?

The hibiscus outside a sliding door is the end of a margin.

Purgatory is a cleansing through counting, let the choral songs begin. Get those numbers off me. Better to be the dancing people, the ones who drew neither numbers nor words but listened to music and moved. When I think of people as midges or masses, I want to kill them, but if I see a face up close I love it. I lost a person, the person lost me, we never met again, it was the beginning of time and only thirty years have passed. I have to give in to the absolute. The pleasure of relativity was minor and each fact was as alike as not. It's time to change. I have had an incredibly good life. They didn't skimp, were generous with the details.

Whether by magic or medics, it is a rule that you should behave like the majority. People make fun of imagination. I don't know how this happened, the joke of everything alien. I want to tell you that my daughter has been better company than any fellow citizen. I never really liked to let her out of the house.

I think I was God.

As Like As Not

The more you keep moving, the more you divide. With each new step, you leave a portion behind.

One time I was struck from behind. Hit, with commitment, as if I were an obstacle and needed to know about it.

When someone hits you and you find your head falling towards the ground at a rate you have only dreamed of, you often will put out your hands too late to stop the blow. This is when you are holding a sandwich you don't want to injure.

However I held nothing. The pummeling I received on the head from behind brought all of me down. Legs and elbows and empty hands. I smelled the sparkling stone but my main sensation was aural. What a murmuring temple we inhabit!

I heard the water gurgling under the pavement while a white fruit tree slowly came to light, bobbing its wings against brick. What I then saw shocked me. My body, male and aged, lay on a paved road and then began to rise. Pellets of hail ticked through white blossoms like hardened pollen.

Climbing to my feet I saw a wretched man walking full-speed across the heath in the direction of the tea shop. His view from himself, backwards, to me, mirrored my own view looking forwards at him, our eyes like four pierced wounds.

Now he rubbed the nob on the base of his skull and his lips curled.
He had walked here, I am sure, because the place reminded him of some-where better. He joined droves of uprooted persons whose drift across the earth made them into pilgrims who worshipped their own perceptions and memories. Portable shrines, their bodies exulted in the mystery of identity.

He was a creature of minimal distinction. Shabbily dressed, hairline receding. Every article of clothing was worn only for comfort. He was a proletarian drudge, like one who had carried wheelbarrows of sod over bumpy fields for generations, but now was stuck in a forty-hour-a-week desk job. Only dogs took note of him and rushed up to greet him on this walk. He murmured to them politely, almost obsequiously.

Screams blasted from outside the tea shop. A mad girl was there accompanied by a young attendant. Every Tuesday it was the same story. The girl slapped herself in the face and shrieked, then pounded every tree trunk and wall with her fists, twisted around and pointed a stiff accusing finger at the sky.

This girl was one of the people who suffer inconsolable terror from the moment of their birth. They contain enough suffering for several hundred people. I saw, from where I knelt, the man enter the tea shop and the shop girl steaming the bags inside the tin pot, then filling it with milk and water.

When the man sat down he was facing a forsythia bush across the path and the mad girl and her attendant. His back was turned to the biscuits and Cadbury's chocolates, gateaux and soft puddings. He liked to sit where he could eye the mad girl free of charge for only fifty pence and that included a cup of tea.

When he allowed himself, he succumbed to sounds of lorries and other engines, buses and voices. It put him into a soporific state while he watched that child's tragic fate unfolding before him.

This man once (in another life) inhabited a woman's body. She had day work as a launderer for a hotel as small as a B & B. She stripped the beds, carried the loads of wash to the launderette, watched them whirl, dried them, returned and made the beds by 11 a.m. each day. Minimum wage, but it kept her going in a pleasingly sleepy state associated with sheets and pillowcases.

He didn't remember that she lived in a basement bed-sit, dirt cheap and dirty too, try as she might to keep it clean. Loneliness? Nothing owed, nothing owned.

Here it was raining, there it was shining, and the tattered shrubs that lined the walk through the heath were showing buttercup yellow buds. Sweet bits of paper wrapping glittered in the muck. The mad girl was tearing at her face, her female attendant was indifferent.

Mothers and children passed by in procession. Step by step, they gathered the pieces of themselves together.

One day one of the hotel maids turned to her and said, "Let's pretend an hour of work is worth the wage they pay us for it." Red lipstick speckled the top of the broomstick she had just sucked. A near drizzle held all parts of the city together.

Ice floes, resembling appliances, had long since split apart and melted. In a minute the other maids were tucking white aprons over their white uniforms, and one of them saw the airport as a scab being eaten by flying insects. She stared at its towers whenever she ate.

This applesauce is perfectly salted, one of them remarked.

Another one pretended her tray was a raft in the dishwater. And a third thought about brown pennies being "extras" just the way she, with her brown skin, was considered extra.

Stay alert, muttered the laundry maid, putting her tray down gingerly. A man might come along.

At this hour every day she dialed World War One-One-One on the phone. It was the hour when a blue trim appeared along the tops of the buildings and filled in the spaces between them and branches. And while the voice of the operator called to her to respond, she didn't say a word. It was 7 a.m. in Dubrovnik.

The streets were empty the way they can be on Sundays in any city. But no one was going to church anymore. The air was heavy, gray as an old tire tread.

Only the truly flat-out and broken people believed that G-d cared for them. They were crushed into silver foil in the fist of their maker.

On a radio the verdict was in. Mary did appear in Medjugorge, predicting war in the months to come, months built like pyramids out of mass, anonymous activities. Clambering humans would orchestrate results in an atmosphere of ever-opening skies of science.

Experiment would replace experience. But Mary was a virgin, a mother and the sister of clairvoyance.

The broom-sweeping launderer saw the man of her dreams on his way to the men's room.

In the temple of the Lord, everyone was complaining.

I will never love anyone as much as I love him, she whispered. I wish I didn't have the curse.

I once knew a man who was INSANE. His face looked as if it was pressed against glass, but orange glass. He had difficulty smiling. Yeah yeah yeah, he muttered impatiently instead. He squinted out to sea in the middle of the city. He could never hide his feelings, he had lost ALL HOPE. We were all in danger of losing our minds when he was in charge of arranging the vegetables in front of the store, he was so slow & clumsy! But then he could be really kind —

Male or Female

I think I remember that night so well when we slept outdoors, because I, for the first time, was privy to the mystery of indifference.

That is, I was interchangeable with you, as a servant is named a servant only because of the boss, I was both text and textile.

Even cold water is not indifferent. You can swim in it and it will change form to accommodate you. It feels you as much as you feel it.

But human indifference is a mystery and a window into the true state of things on earth and in the starry climes. Your indifference was in that cosmic category.

From where I stand the drop to the ground is forty feet. Bushes below, a cement path.

Do other planets share their genes and feelings?
Do you know Teresa's System?
The salt in the sea contributes to the sand and to the clay in cliffs.
The window into the true state of things is made of salt, sand, they become like fly wings.
The other side of the window is another time.
You leave your legs behind and nail them to the floor.
I have become your color, the way a jewel is on skin. So don't move.

Your aura, your soul-tone, is orange. But your skin is like clay.
This creates a problem in your ability to change. In the bed twice, suicide was a temptation. But I saw each time through the window remembering.
A jumping dance around a tiny living room. Coat thrown down.

Hot cheeks and necking in movie theaters with broken seats and restored reels.
Words, dog, leaves on a summer table, weeping without being seen.
I know that the woman who threw herself out of a hotel window did so because you were late. Not just a little late, but two days late.

So tonight I will think about the politics of indifference because it is near-ly suicide on Memorial Drive.

Please
re-dream [...]|c 55°
my Book-[...] skate-boarding
cat[...] in Weimar.
[...] sleep
Heaven [...] God (and others)
What all [that] time?
Go° War-dogs!
There were times before
when it was better — One
Time and the SENTENCE. attempt.

Please
re-dream [...]|c 55°
my Book-[...] skate-boarding
cat[...] in Weimar.
[...] sleep
Heaven [...] God (and others)
What all [that] time?
Go° War-dogs!
There were times before
when it was better — One
Time and the SENTENCE. attempt.

The window is six inches from my foot and open.

All attitudes and events are interconnected.

In the office of the President, they are wondering:
Why not kill everyone? Why not destroy the world? Why wait for the inevitable end? Why suffer through it all? Why work for minimum wage? Why not let the winners make all the decisions? Why worry about someone you don't know? Why have children? Why study and produce? Why not imprison or shoot all social failures?

This is what I hear every time I phone you:

"I'm not available for your call right now. Please leave a message."

So I will never leave you a message. Because it is the space between us that has to be protected.
Not the lonely message.

When you and I were alive in the sheets, we wanted to know each other's feelings, not our own.
And when you abandoned me, I believed that I had done something wrong. Then I became a worse version of the one you had left, because added to that version was a monster in active unbelief.

I was deprived of any virtue except in solitude.

Soldier, slave, when I welcomed you back, it was an attempt at filling in the terrible space of unmeaning.

But you had left me because I loved you.

You sought peace for yourself but not for me. You called it peace as anyone with power will do, when walking away with the spoils.

How would we avoid this injustice? Only by speech. By each of us telling the other that our past together was a great pain and a great joy that would never be erased.

Psychology can depoliticize experience. A wounded person wants to talk about obligations, not about masochism. The body count after a war is nothing compared to all the uncounted ties and lost ones between the people who remain living.

I can never go back to my homeland to live but have been driven from there by the city's consciousness of my failure.

It adheres to the river, bridge, brick and granite gravestones.

In that city nobody loved me or gave me a job. Winners stuck with their plans and stayed in one place, and those whose hearts were strong didn't notice the problems that might weaken them.

A tent and bags inside a park.

Ice crisp on the canvas. Two cousins, man and woman, sleeping there.

Institutions but few such asylums as that one.
A lost water tower spackled with graffiti on a mental hospital's grounds.
Dog, watery spikes, and a van.
I can never go back to my homeland except at the end.

So let us kiss and part. In other words, be equals and friends.

Out there the pharmacist is a woman measuring pills and powders. Anti-depressants counted by a stranger's hands or a bar where working life is laughed over. Mental activities awash in emotion and moralizing. Give me my meds, imperialist over what I am permitted to put into myself.

If there is no other way to remove an obstacle to peace except war, then war is said to be just. So if there is unquenchable bitterness and anger in a people you probably have the duty to exterminate them.
People who have encountered indifference will often want to kill or be killed.
Can you say that what follows is called peace? It's true that peace is the absence of anger and bitterness, and the absence of the people who felt those feelings. So then they should be killed to get to peace?

People sometimes select and seduce someone who reminds them of someone else, so that then they can damage the person who is not the original. Just in case the original decides to come back and love them.

No one I know can kill without being able to justify the act because we all want the good or at least to be associated with the good.

"Hey, I know that ant."
Have you ever heard a pilot say that?
People say about other people, They all look alike. This is a warning that the look-alikes are going to be killed.

Being forsaken by someone is like walking into a basement, as I once did, in a building devoted to science, and coming upon a room full of corpses with their knees pointing up to the ceiling under their sheets, and wondering if this was the peace you were seeking.
They all looked alike.
It was similar to the experience of coming upon the same word being used to define itself in a dictionary and then another and another after, until they all devolved into one word and that word had no name.

My Last Life

There's a goat's hair in the soldier's tea. The soldier is me. It's the last straw, so to speak. Over my head there is only one mothering image on the wall. A woman with bosom and baby sucking on it. Mary, I suppose.

Outside there is that staccato background sound of a city corner. Fart-like hissing from trucks. Dublin's Daily Bread is written on one of them. The tree's leaves are like sheaves of light, the green barely visible. A pear bud kills its pear by making it too heavy for the branch to bear.

I head away from my plane. Anterior to the airport is an ugly church, a circuit road and an Archbishop's residence surrounded by a wall. Suburban housing, children in blue uniforms, the sun is blazing. Yellow leaves drift to the bench where I sit. The ozone hole dilates near the north pole, I suppose, thanks to the airplane fumes trailing over the clouds.

An old telephone pole blackens the estuary surface. Like a photograph and a negative at the same time. Ripples filter to a pebbled bank. Here a memory of war, there a memory of dogs. Nostalgia is dangerous. In Dublin the people are women, the same old workers of the world there always were, thick across the abdomen and strong from lifting goods out of bags for generations.

Nobody is doing too well financially. Newspapers cost a lot and young adults are on the dole, strolling around plate glass windows with the thin anxious faces of brokers. There is a scraped socialist feeling to the walls and sidewalks. Everywhere you look, you wonder how long the world can last.

I will tell you now Mrs. O'Toole will suffer multiple head wounds only yards away from her semi-detached home. Highlights blond in her useless hair. Spanish style ruins are being constructed in the next neighborhood with the somber thumps of all such constructions around the world. Even as her murderer approaches her, me, more glorious sunshine causes the board of management for primary schools to be merciful. During the holidays it lashed rain, but now the sun is hot. Teachers (of whom Mrs. O'Toole is one) are permitted to let the children leave early.

Within a mile of where she will die, a Druid armchair burns from the sun. More and more splendid and indifferent sunshine. An Orangeman emerges from negotiations with a Green, assuring his men that he is only sympathetic to Protestants, not to worry. A body is lured into a Chinese restaurant in Belfast before it is shot. Mrs. O'Toole's bank is called "the people's choice for a personal debt" and she takes out some money.

The happy fact is that she left school early today, just like the children in her class. She is off to visit the Martello tower where her favorite sweets are for sale and she can watch the sea like a movie while she eats. High wall gone low and the pink house facing Howth, where she spent a happy summer, was now painted yellow. A little dog is still sleeping against the stones and people are swimming with colored caps on their heads.
When the train zooms alongside the back gardens, she thinks the world seems doomed, but she shapes up her own face anyway in the tiny compact her husband gave her, saying the mirror O stands for Rebirth. He is a poet at work in Dundrum.

Petunias coil gentian around a tree. Wild geese follow the mist west. No one can be sure if love is true, but from above the tininess of humanity does not increase any belief at all. I should know, from my time in boot camp. To astrologers, this is the time called Loss of Illusion. I couldn't help admiring Mrs. O'Toole's artificial highlights. I, being nearly a boy still, just a soldier down from the north for a day and night of fun, got drunk and then killed her. The crime will give me time in jail to get tired of life fast, said to be a blessing.

When we finally begin to talk, she doesn't know I've been following her since we both got off the train at Seapoint. Lav, hydrangea, wooden bench. Walls sticky with vines and clothesline vestments bulging in sunlight. She tells me when I ask that she isn't absolutely sure it was such a happy summer she spent in that yellow house after all.

That's retrospect for you, I say.
Her face turned to me and embarrassed me with its nudity. Really, veils make sense to me. Unconventional women with their faces wide open, no, all women, even the most bourgeois, well, their naked faces fill me with shame for them.
Once you've really seen a woman's face, there's nothing left to wonder about, I told her.

Put us in convents or jails where the walls will take care of this issue? Is that what you had in mind, boy?

We stare away from each other. Delivery concludes. A horse wagon continues clopping towards Dublin. Cars, with nothing to replace them possible. This is the case with capitalism, waste, because no mutations. Something dumb like equality for the lucky.

Democracy isn't an ideology the way they want it to be. Fate's not waiting but working.

No wonder, given. Yes, the whole human face should be hidden, even the eyes, just the way the sexual organs is. Too much showing as is. And no pity for any of it. Of the limits of what we should know. Everyone's plum interior, especially a woman's, is best left secret. My favorite smell goes back to a pot of porridge, the smell of tar but the color of thick white stuff, dripping and sticking like a pudding to a spoon.

I recommend leaving memories behind, boy, says Mrs. O'Toole.

This is the way a painful word can derange the air around it. It has no unifying shape.

The interior life of the speaker is then displayed on the screen as something broken, or burned. What held the plot together is now tossed into the database of hell. It hurts to watch or to hear. I once loved someone who didn't love me back. Every word she uttered was saturated in meaning, negative meaning.

Now I lied to her. A choice very Irish. I said, "I am not a boy."

Two clouds were impressed on blue sky as solitary wanderers, white sheep lost from their shepherd. Years of women carried from the beach.

There was a pub and this is the drunk part. Will always be the cause. Later berries will be crushed under Mrs. O'Toole's shoulderblades. A slice of palm. All roads lead to home and so do all surfaces, rough or tall, lead to the sun. The woman will run in that direction where it is now setting in the west, all the while me saying, "God, I've come a long way from being crazy the way I was. When I was dispersed my soul split into parts outside my body and no one was recognizable, not even Mum, monsters all, and even she was the enemy of hope. Now I am in uniform so I can feel I am the same as everyone. Bombs, lambs, what's the difference in the end. I can reach out and actually cover another face with my hand. Lips and tongue will be buried in my own skin. So let her bite me. Without pain, I will die of loneliness. But with pleasure, I will too. Be it then both."

A Murmuring Temple

When It was still a baby and the world was in agony, its mother was taken from It. It was flown first to Finland, and then driven around mountains by a group of nuns.

Now the miracle of mechanical engineering had introduced a clatter of contradictory signals. Satellites were a major factor in the confusion. In order to clear things up, prisoners of war experienced some form of torture from beating or electric shock, while women and children were often subjected to mental torture and rape, instead.

During that time several messages were transmitted through its ears simultaneously. Sorry It doesn't remember them or why any of this happened. Years later, working hard during the day, It often failed to refer its mind to the present, and returned, by chance, to that furious zone. Its only way to break the clamor was to listen to music or a bird and this way locate the comfort of harmony, It who had a deep-seated fear of chaos.

In those days the maker of newfangled instruments was like a merchant in a toyshop with his toys strung up in sales tags, and the name of the game was nano-technology. He was an atom-mover and his analogies would lead you farther and farther from experience. Since that time the same kinds of makers deal in numbers and abstractions and predictions and guesses. They rule the world.

They better beware because conversion to God through money is impossible, since the permanent destruction of hope trails an abstract system—Hell which is cold all over and shapeless as a bombed ceiling is made of such indifference.

It was exported, finally, not for insubordination or race like the grown-ups but because of innocence. In order to preserve its infancy the nuns knocked the soldiers clear into the air. They smashed lead crystal lamps and bent solid brass in their fury. Without one compassionate thought, they became akin to their own enemy. With wheels and connectors, they turned into a train rumbling around collecting human toys like It. With their wheels removed, they built stackable bodies inside a freighter that crossed the sea. It was their own foolishness at taking vows of poverty, chastity, and obedience that saved them and It and other children in the end. The sisters were brave. They understood that a soul has to live in order to be saved.

About the Author

Fanny Howe is the author of more than twenty books of poetry and prose, including most recently the novel *Indivisible*, the book of poetry *On the Ground*, and a book of essays *The Wedding Dress: Meditations on Word and Life*. Professor Emerita of Writing and Literature at the University of California, San Diego, she now lives in Massachusetts.

About Nightboat Books

Nightboat Books, a nonprofit organization, seeks to develop audiences for writers whose work resists convention and transcends boundaries by publishing books rich with poignancy, intelligence, and risk.

The following individuals have supported the publication of this book. We thank them for their generosity and commitment to the mission of Nightboat Books:

Meghan Adler
Nick and Suzanne Chapis
Kathleen Ellis
Brenda Gold and Dale Wozny
Brian Goldfaden and Nicole DuBois
Josh Goldfaden
Lois Hirshkowitz

Sarah Heller
Ruth Lepson
Daniel Lin
Juliet Patterson
Evelyn Reilly
Jonathan C. Randal
Anonymous (3)

Please visit our website www.nightboat.org to find out how you can support future publications of Nightboat Books.

Forthcoming in March 2006

The Truant Lover by Juliet Patterson
Winner of the 2005 Nightboat Poetry Prize, chosen by Jean Valentine

> "Juliet Patterson's poems are entirely themselves; they use time and the eye and tongue—all the body, as thought and insight, inside and outside history. *The Truant Lover* is a marvel."
> —Jean Valentine